# Do Plants Really Eat Insects?

Thomas Canavan

W

FRANKLIN WATTS
LONDON·SYDNEY

First published in 2013 by Franklin Watts

Franklin Watts
338 Euston Road
London
NW1 3BH

Franklin Watts Australia
Level 17/207 Kent Street, Sydney, NSW 2000

Produced by Arcturus Publishing Limited,
26/27 Bickels Yard, 151–153 Bermondsey Street, London SE1 3HA

Editor: Joe Harris
Picture researcher: Joe Harris
Designer: Ian Winton

Picture credits: All images supplied by Shutterstock except page 6b: Bennett Dean/Eye Ubiquitous/ Corbis and page 26t: Xinhua Press/Corbis.

A CIP catalogue record for this book is available from the British Library.

Dewey Decimal Classification Number: 580

ISBN: 978 1 4451 2237 3

Franklin Watts is a division of Hachette Children's Books, an Hachette UK company.
www.hachette.co.uk

Printed in China

SL002503EN
Supplier 03, Date 0513 Print Run 2361

# Contents

# It's a jungle out there!

Nearly everywhere you look you see plants – sometimes so many that it would be impossible to count them all. But just how much do you know about all of these green inhabitants of planet Earth?

## Are tomatoes fruits or vegetables?

Even some scientists disagree about this. The simple answer is that tomatoes are fruits. Why? Because scientists define a fruit as the mature ovary of a plant, containing seeds. All the other parts of a plant – such as leaves (e.g. lettuce), stems (e.g. celery) and roots (e.g. carrots) are called vegetables.

## Can you eat flowers?

You certainly can! In fact, you may have eaten some this week if you've had broccoli or cauliflower. These are the flowering parts of plants. Many attractive flowers, such as violets and roses, can also be eaten or used to make teas. But it's important to remember that some flowers are poisonous, and we should never simply assume that a flower is edible.

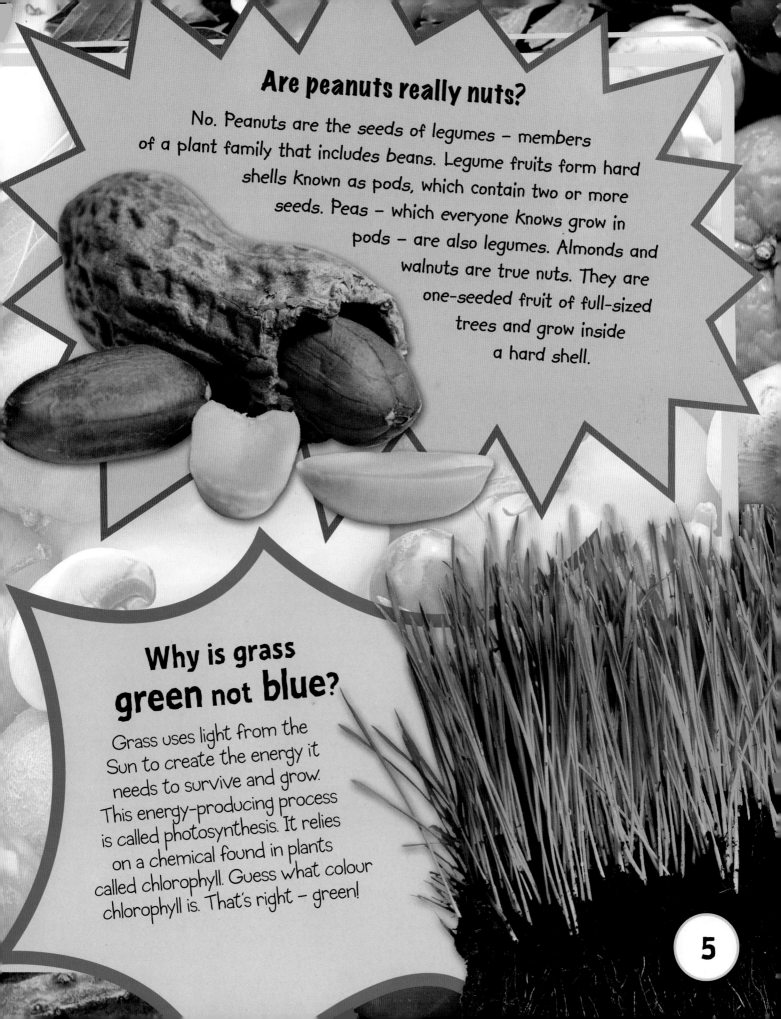

## Are peanuts really nuts?

No. Peanuts are the seeds of legumes – members of a plant family that includes beans. Legume fruits form hard shells known as pods, which contain two or more seeds. Peas – which everyone knows grow in pods – are also legumes. Almonds and walnuts are true nuts. They are one-seeded fruit of full-sized trees and grow inside a hard shell.

## Why is grass green not blue?

Grass uses light from the Sun to create the energy it needs to survive and grow. This energy-producing process is called photosynthesis. It relies on a chemical found in plants called chlorophyll. Guess what colour chlorophyll is. That's right – green!

# Try this for size

Plants can range in size from tiny speck-like seeds to towering giant redwoods. And the more you find out about them, the more they will grow on you!

## Is it really possible to drive a car through a tree?

Yes. In the giant redwood and sequoia forests of northern California there are several trees that have been hollowed out so that cars can drive through them. One of the most famous is 96 m (315 ft) tall. A road passes through a hole in the trunk that is 1.83 m (6 ft) wide and 2.06 m (6 ft, 9 in) high.

## What is the largest fruit in the world?

The jackfruit tree produces a fruit that weighs more than many ten-year-olds. It grows in the rainforests of India and South-east Asia. The fruits can be 90 cm (36 in) long, 47 cm (19 in) wide and weigh up to 36 kg (80 lb). They taste like sour banana.

## Which plant has the largest seeds?

The world's largest seed comes from the Coco de Mer. This is a type of palm tree that is native to islands in the Indian Ocean. Its seeds form inside giant egg-shaped fruit. These can weigh more than 17 kg (37 lb).

## Can corn really grow 'as high as an elephant's eye'?

This is a line from a famous American song – but is it just a tall tale? Most elephants' eyes are about 3 m (10ft) off the ground, and most corn is harvested when it is about 2.5 m (8 ft) tall. But with enough rain, sunshine and fertilizer, corn can grow up to 4 m (13 ft) or even higher. So in fact, corn can grow even taller than an elephant's eye!

# Peckish plants

'Water! Water! I need water!' Was that someone stranded in the desert... or was it the houseplant that you forgot to water? Plants need water and food just as much as we do, and they have some funny ways of getting to them.

## Do some plants really eat insects?

Most plants get enough nutrients from the soil to survive and grow. Some plants that live in areas with poor soil rely on insects as part of their 'diet'. The leaves of a Venus Flytrap, for example, open out like the pages of a book. Inside are sensitive hairs. If an insect lands on a hair, the leaves snap shut. The leaves then release chemicals to digest the insect.

## Which plants drink the most water?

Trees can survive without rain for a long time, but only if their roots can draw up water from sources underground. Douglas firs grow in areas with low rainfall. They can suck up more than 800 litres (176 gallons) of water a day after a sudden rainstorm.

# Do plants poo?

The scientific name for pooing is excretion. Our bodies excrete (get rid of) waste after we digest food. Plants make their own food through photosynthesis. Plant cells store waste in pocket-like spaces called vacuoles. Some scientists believe that trees can also get rid of poisons by storing them in leaves and bark that will fall off naturally.

# Can you make a flower change colour?

Yes. The colour of a blossom can depend on the minerals in the soil where it grows. Florists can change the colour of some flowers by adding colouring to the water they use. In science experiments students can add food colouring to water to change the appearance of carnations and other flowers.

# Jobs to do

Imagine a sergeant barking out these orders. 'Flowers – attract some insects. Roots – we need more water. Thorns – keep those deer away!' Each part of a plant really does have a job to do, even if no one's there to order it around.

## Why do some trees have needles instead of leaves?

The needles of evergreen trees are really leaves. Like other leaves, they contain chlorophyll, the green chemical that helps plants make their own food. Evergreens grow where it is either dry or cold. Their narrow, hard needles lose less water from evaporation than normal leaves. Their long, thin shape also protects them from the extreme cold.

## What's the 'point' of thorns?

Plants have no way of escaping from hungry animals looking for tasty leaves or blossoms for their next meal. That's why some plants, such as roses and cacti, grow thorns as a form of self-defence. A deer might think twice about sticking its delicate nose through a bunch of thorns just to reach a tasty rosebud.

## Do a tree's roots grow as deep downwards as the tree grows upwards?

Most tree roots are surprisingly shallow. Even some of the tallest trees have roots that go down less than 45 cm (18 in). Trees can be blown over in strong winds because they don't have deep roots to anchor them. Although the roots are shallow, they can be wide. Some root networks are three times as wide as the branches above.

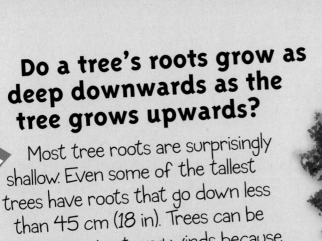

## Why do trees have bark?

Trees and shrubs actually have two layers of bark. The inner layer is made up of long, tube-like cells called xylem. They transport water and minerals up from the roots. The outer layer is made up of dead cells. These cells have hardened to form a protective barrier against insects. They also stop water from the inner bark evaporating.

# Birds and bees... and trees

Just like humans, plants produce offspring and do their best to make sure the next generation grows up to be healthy. They have some clever ways to do this.

## Why do bees love flowers?

Flowers produce nectar, a sweet juicy liquid that attracts bees. The bees collect nectar and use it to make honey. But what's in it for the flowers? Well, a fine powder called pollen sticks to the bees while they collect the nectar. The busy bees visit lots of flowers. The pollen from one flower combines with the pollen from another flower to allow seeds to form.

## How long can an acorn survive before it has to be planted?

A fully grown oak produces up to 30,000 acorns a year. But not all will grow into new trees. Some acorns last through a winter – or even two winters – before they germinate (start to grow). Gardeners can store acorns for up to three years as long as they don't get too wet, dry, hot or cold.

## How do farmers help crops to grow well?

Many farmers add factory-made chemicals to soil or spray them on plants to protect crops from weeds, insects and other pests. Some farmers avoid factory-made chemicals and use more natural methods. For example, they use manure to nourish the soil, or plant other crops that pests don't like. This is called organic farming.

ORGANIC

## What are those little helicopters that float down from sycamore trees each autumn?

They're seeds. Plants use lots of ways to spread their seeds in order to make more plants. Sycamores use a really surprising method. Each sycamore seed comes packed in its own 'helicopter'. When it's ripe, it is ready to be blown off the tree and carried by the wind to a new growing spot.

# Peculiar plants

Do you think that plants just sit there and don't do much? You'll know better once you get to know these weirdos. You might want to stand back or even hold your nose!

## Do Mexican jumping beans really **jump**?

Yes, they really do bounce, but they're not really beans, and it's not the plant that's doing the jumping. The larva of a small moth eats into the seed casing of a Mexican shrub. Protected from the desert sun, it grows into an adult moth. But if it feels too warm inside, it swings to try and move into the shade. And that makes the 'bean' seem to jump.

## Why do nettles sting?

Nettles sting for the same reason that some plants have thorns: to protect themselves. Nettle flowers are protected from plant-eating mammals by the stinging leaves all around them. However, insects are still able to land on the flowers and carry away their pollen, so that the nettles can reproduce.

## What is the smelliest fruit?

The durian grows in South-east Asia and looks a bit like a large, thorny pineapple. But its smell is what makes the durian famous. It's been described as a cross between rotten onions and dirty gym socks! Some people actually like the smell and describe the durian as the 'King of fruits'.

## Why do some cacti only bloom for one day a year?

The Purple Ball Cactus needs to attract insects to its flowers in order to reproduce. However, a delicate bloom like a rose or tulip would shrivel in the desert heat. The cactus solves this problem by making a flower with a protective waxy covering. However, it takes a lot of effort to make this flower... so much, that it only blooms for one day a year!

15

# Changing nature

Plants were around for millions of years before the first humans showed up. But ever since we've discovered them we've been changing them; their colour, their size and even their genes.

## Which plants did the first human farmers grow?

Scientists are looking for evidence of when humans first began farming. In 2006, scientists uncovered a collection of 11,300-year-old figs along with human remains in Israel. The figs were a type that needed to be planted – not just picked. Another recent find, in Korea, suggests that farmers might have been growing rice 15,000 years ago.

## Why are bonsai trees so small?

Bonsai is the Japanese art of training small trees and shrubs to look like fully grown trees. Their owners trim and prune small branches to make them grow in this unusual way. Most bonsai ('tray-planted') trees are only about 50 cm (20 in) tall.

## Why are carrots orange?

Until the late 1600s, carrots could be purple, white, red or yellow. According to one theory, today's orange carrots are descendants of the 'Long Orange Dutch Carrot', which was first described in 1721. This was created by Dutch farmers who were looking for a way to honour their leader William of Orange. They cross-bred different carrot varieties until they found a hardy orange variety.

## What are GM crops?

Some scientists are working to alter the genes in plants to make them more productive or better able to resist pests. Plants that have been modified (changed) like this are called Genetically Modified (GM) crops. But there's a big debate about the effects of GM crops on the environment.

# Going to extremes

We humans can survive in baking deserts or freezing polar regions and we have even travelled to the Moon. Plants can live in some extreme places, too...

## Can plants grow at the North or South poles?

No plants can grow at the North or South Poles because the temperatures are so cold all year. A few plants manage to survive in the Arctic region near the North Pole and the Antarctic region near the South Pole. These tend to be simple plants like moss, or tough grasses.

## Does a cactus have any leaves?

Its leaves, called spines, look like sharp needles. A leaf shaped like an oak or beech leaf would shrivel up in the hot desert sun. The spines protect the cactus against plant-eating animals.

## Why are there no trees on Mount Everest and other high mountains?

The air temperature goes down the higher up you climb. The temperature on the highest mountains is around -40° C (-40° F). High winds, even on lower mountains, blow soil away so that only rock remains. These conditions are no good for plants.

## Do plants grow on any other planets?

So far scientists have found no evidence of any type of life on other planets. Most are either too hot or too cold. US scientists have sent a robot vehicle, called Curiosity, to study Mars. It might find evidence that plants did grow there long ago, when the planet's atmosphere was more like ours.

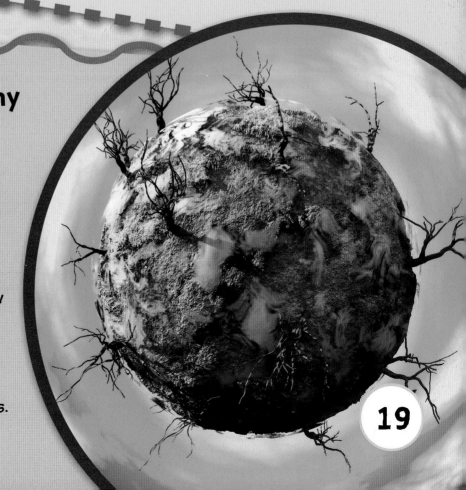

# Get a life!

'Life goes on', and on and on for plants. Some of them patiently grow for years – almost 5,000 years in some cases. They'll grow almost anywhere and while growing, they go through all sorts of changes.

## Why do some leaves change colour and fall in the autumn?

Leaves don't really 'change colour' – they just lose their strong green colour. This lets other colours (which had been hidden all along) show themselves. In cold weather a layer of cells blocks the water tubes in the leaves to protect the tree from frost. That causes the colourful leaves to dry up and then fall each autumn.

## How old are the world's oldest trees?

High in the White Mountains of eastern California is a group of bristlecone pines. Most of these trees are well over 4,000 years old. Many would have started growing more than 1,400 years before the pyramids of Egypt were built. The oldest bristlecone, called Methuselah (after the oldest person in the Bible), is 4,844 years old.

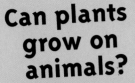

## Can plants grow on animals?

True plants cannot grow on animals, but some plant-like organisms do make their homes on animals. Most are types of algae, which are able to produce their own food (like plants) but lack leaves, roots or stems. One-celled algae called diatoms live in the skin of many whales. They don't feed on the whales, but nourish themselves with seawater.

## How do plants know which way is up?

Plants – even seeds – contain a chemical called auxin, which directs their growth. The two important directions are up (towards light) and down (towards water). Auxin causes the stem cells to grow upwards and the root cells to grow downwards.

21

# Power plants

Just about everything you touch, see or eat has some sort of connection with the plant world. That connection helps us tick...and move around...and stay warm...and makes us better when we're not well.

## Can you run a car on **sugar** instead of **petrol?**

Yes – sugar can be turned into a type of alcohol called ethanol, which some cars can use as fuel. Brazil is the world's largest producer of sugar, and 13 million Brazilian cars can run on ethanol. The world is running out of oil, the source of petrol. Ethanol supplies, however, can be replaced just by planting more sugarcane.

## What is herbal medicine?

Herbal medicine uses the bark, leaves, roots and flowers of plants to treat illness. This form of medicine has been used for thousands of years. Many herbal cures contain the same helpful chemicals as those used in modern medicine, but in smaller amounts.

## Could you live in a house made of grass?

Yes, you could, and many people do! Bamboo is a strong, fast-growing type of grass and a useful building material. It is surprisingly strong and has beaten oak and even steel in some tests. Bamboo houses have been popular throughout Asia for hundreds of years. Builders in other parts of the world are now using it to make bridges, floors and roofs.

## Which tree produces the strongest timber?

Timber experts use denting to compare how hard different woods are. The Janka hardness test measures the force needed to press a small steel ball halfway into a piece of wood. The hardest wood is the Australian bull oak. Using the Janka test, it is about 50 times harder than balsa, one of the softest woods.

# Eat your greens!

Plants have a starring role whenever it's time for us to eat – from the tastiest tuck-shop chocolate to the slimiest portion of spinach on your school-dinner plate.

## Does spinach really make you **strong**?

For years, people believed that spinach made you strong because it contains a lot of iron (which strengthens muscles). In reality spinach has no more iron than most other green vegetables. It is still good for you though. The vitamins it contains protect the heart, bones and eyes.

## Are green potatoes really poisonous?

Green potatoes contain a poison called solanine, which makes you feel ill and gives you bad headaches. Potatoes make solanine when they are exposed to warmth and light. Warmth and light also lead the potato to produce chlorophyll. So it's the green chlorophyll that's the clue that there is poison in the potato.

## Could a plant grow in your tummy if you swallowed a seed?

Luckily, this is not a problem. Think about what plants need to survive – water, carbon dioxide, light and nutrients from soil. Of these, only water could be available in your tummy, and even then it would be mixed with some strong acid. So the conditions just aren't right for growing plants in your stomach.

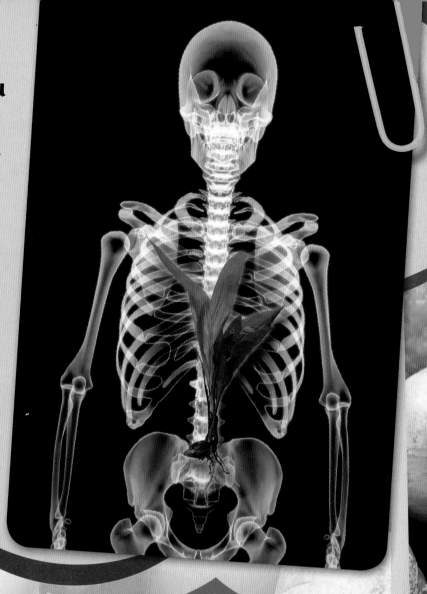

## Where does chocolate come from?

Chocolate comes from the beans (or 'seeds') of the cacao tree. These beans are left in pots to ferment and become less bitter. Then they are roasted and their outer shells are removed. What's left, the 'nibs', are crushed into a paste. Chocolate makers then mix in sugar, vanilla and milk. The paste is mashed for days and then heated several times. The result is delicious chocolate.

# Don't be so wet!

Every plant needs water to survive but that usually means taking it in — not living in it. Here are some plants that really make a splash.

## Can you really sit on a lily pad?

You can't sit on just any waterlily, but some tropical species are large enough to hold a young child. The giant waterlily of the Amazon region produces more than 40 leaves, which rest on the calm water surface. The leaves grow up to 2.5 m (8 ft) across and can support up to 45 kg (100 lb) without sinking.

## Is seaweed a **plant?**

The answer is 'almost'. Seaweed is a type of algae. Like plants, it can create its own food using photosynthesis. Unlike plants, seaweed has no roots or tubes running through it to deliver food and water. That's because every part of it is touching water and able to make food, so there's no need for a system of 'pipes'.

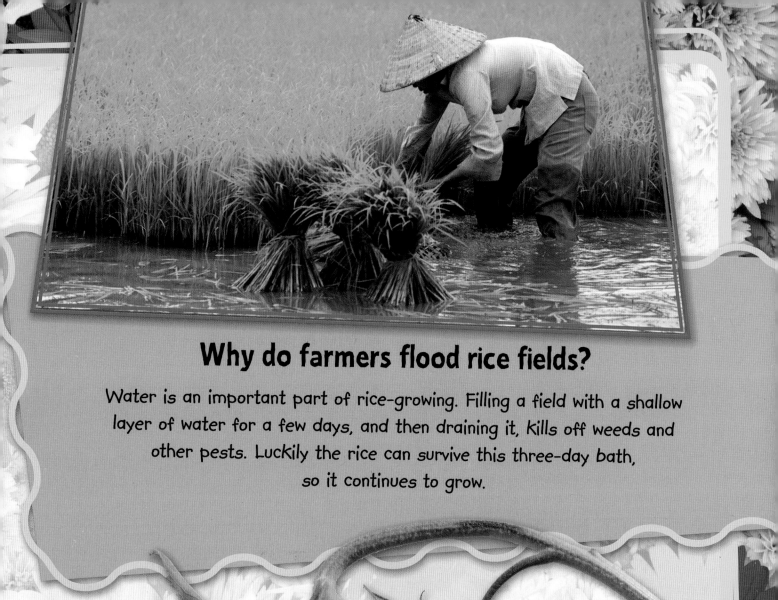

# Why do farmers flood rice fields?

Water is an important part of rice-growing. Filling a field with a shallow layer of water for a few days, and then draining it, kills off weeds and other pests. Luckily the rice can survive this three-day bath, so it continues to grow.

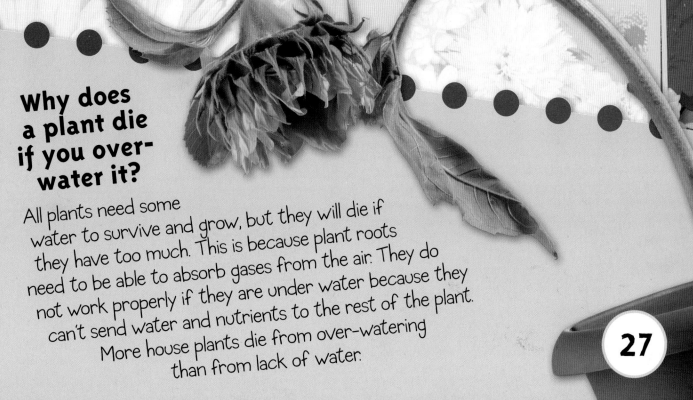

## Why does a plant die if you over-water it?

All plants need some water to survive and grow, but they will die if they have too much. This is because plant roots need to be able to absorb gases from the air. They do not work properly if they are under water because they can't send water and nutrients to the rest of the plant. More house plants die from over-watering than from lack of water.

# Just wondering

Do you feel like a plant expert yet? Here are four final questions and answers to kick-start your investigations into the amazing world of trees, shrubs, flowers and seeds...

## How much of the world is covered by trees?

About 30 per cent of the world's land is covered by trees. The exact area is about 40 million sq km (15.4 million sq mi). Of course, forests aren't spread evenly across the planet and some people would have to travel hundreds of kilometres just to see one.

## What is the world's **hottest** chilli pepper?

The Scoville scale measures the amount of capsaicin (the chemical that causes the burn) in chillies. Tabasco sauce has a Scoville reading of about 5,500 and a vindaloo curry is roughly 30,000. In 2011, English chilli-grower Gerald Fowler set a new world record with his Naga Viper chilli, which measured 1.3 million Scoville Heat Units!

## What is the world's most poisonous plant?

Most plant experts agree that the castor-oil plant is the deadliest. Its poison, called ricin, is contained in the seeds. Swallowing as few as four of these beans leads to a painful death in about five days unless the person is treated by a doctor.

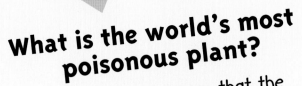

## Are mushrooms plants?

They grow on the ground. People eat them. Mushrooms must be plants, right? The answer is no! Mushrooms lack one of the most important features of plants – the ability to make their own food. Instead, mushrooms get their food from dead and decaying plants, which is why we see them on old tree stumps.

29

# Glossary

**algae** Organisms that can use photosynthesis but which, unlike plants, have no roots, stems or leaves.

**atmosphere** The mixture of gases that forms a layer around Earth and other planets.

**carbon dioxide** A naturally occurring gas that plants use to produce their own food.

**chlorophyll** A green-coloured chemical that plants need for photosynthesis.

**cross-breed** To breed two varieties of a plant or animal to produce offspring with some qualities of each.

**digest** To break down food so that it can be used by the body.

**edible** Able to be eaten by humans.

**evaporation** Turning from a liquid into a gas.

**excretion** When a living creature gets rid of waste.

**fertilizer** Any substance added to soil to make it better for growing plants.

**genetic** Having to do with genes, the substances that cause features to be passed from parents to offspring.

**germinate** To begin growing, especially from a seed.

**herbal** To do with herbs or (discussing medicine) any plants that can be used as cures.

**larva** The worm-like first stage of an insect's life, after it hatches from an egg.

**minerals** Substances in the soil that are neither animal nor plant.

**nutrient** Something that is eaten to promote health and growth.

**ovary** The part of the flower that contains the seeds and grows into a fruit.

**pest** Small creatures that are harmful to crops.

**photosynthesis** The chemical process that plants use to produce food from water, carbon dioxide and light.

**pod** A hard case that contains seeds.

**pollen** A yellow powder produced by a flower to help seeds on other plants become ready for growth.

**rainforest** A thick forest that receives lots of rain all year long.

**reproduce** To have young or offspring.

**root** The part of a plant that grows underground to gather water and nutrients and to anchor the plant to the ground.

**stem** The main part of a plant that grows upwards and supports branches, leaves and flowers.

**vitamin** A nutrient that cannot be produced and must be obtained from other sources.

# Further Reading

*Deserts (Go Facts: Natural Environments)* by Ian Rohr (A & C Black, 2009)

*Kids in the Garden: Growing Plants for Food and Fun* by Elizabeth McCorquodale (Black Dog Publishing, 2010)

*Lost in the Amazon: A Kid's Guide to Surviving in the World's Most Dangerous Rainforest* by Lauri Berkenkamp (Nomad, 2009)

*Plant Cells and Life Processes* by Barbara A. Somervill (Heinemann Library, 2011)

*RHS Ready, Steady, Grow!* by the Royal Horticultural Society (Dorling Kindersley, 2010)

*Scholastic Discover More: Rainforests* by Penelope Arlon (Scholastic Reference, 2013)

# Websites

**Biology4Kids.com**
**www.biology4kids.com/files/plants_main.html**
You can find a wealth of information about the world of plants in this well-designed site that is full of interesting facts, eye-catching images and lively activities.

**The Kids Garden**
**www.thekidsgarden.co.uk/**
This site is about as close as you can get to real gardening without getting your fingers dirty. Puzzles, activities and a range of FAQ sections help provide a wide-ranging resource.

**Plant Interactive Fun for Kids**
**www.vrml.k12.la.us/curriculum/quicktip/science/plants/plants.htm**
This fascinating jumping-off point leads visitors to a wide range of interactive sites dealing with more than a dozen aspects of plant life.

**Royal Horticultural Society**
**www.rhs.org.uk/children**
The children's page of the main RHS site is full of plant-related features and activities. A link takes young gardeners to the Wild About Gardens site run in conjunction with the Wildlife Trusts.

**The Woodland Trust**
**http://www.woodlandtrust.org.uk/en/learning-kids/Pages/children.aspx#.UK9mMKXF-JU**
The Kids and Schools section of the main Woodlands Trust site is full of seasonally adjusted activities and suggestions.

# Index

# Series contents

**SCIENCE F.A.Q.**

**Do Plants Really Eat Insects?** • It's a jungle out there! • Try this for size • Peckish plants • Jobs to do • Birds and bees... and trees • Peculiar plants • Changing nature • Going to extremes • Get a life! • Power plants • Eat your greens! • Don't be so wet! • Just wondering

**Does It Really Rain Frogs?** • Home sweet globe • Stormy weather • Round and round • The right impression • A large shake, please • Forcing the issue • Just give me some time • Lighten up • Making a splash • Rain, rain, go away • Now you've done it • Going to extremes • Air we go

**What Makes You Hiccup?** • It's break time • I beg your pardon • Act your age • Just be sensible • Pick up the pace • Pass it on • Eye eye, sir • Food for thought • Sleep secrets • Hair, there and everywhere • Skin deep • I don't feel well • Anybody's guess

**Why Are Black Holes Black?** • Sunny side up • Meet the neighbours • Hey – lighten up! • Over the moon • Up, up and away • Here comes trouble • Sky-high science • Goin' my way? • Tighten your space helmet • Heavens above • Long ago and far away... • That's life! • It's out of this world

**Why Do Ice Cubes Float?** • Food for thought • Now for some hard questions • It's only natural • It all boils down to science • Pass the gas • Read all about it • Whatever floats your boat • Water wonders • Are you stuck? • That's really cool! • Metal workout • Changing things • Still stumped?

**Why Do Zebras Have Stripes?** • Going for the record • What you see is what you get • All at sea? • Come to your senses • Jurassic park life • Creepy crawlies • Yackety-yak • Baby beasties • What's for dinner? • Up and away • Fact or fiction? • Just like us? • It's round-up time

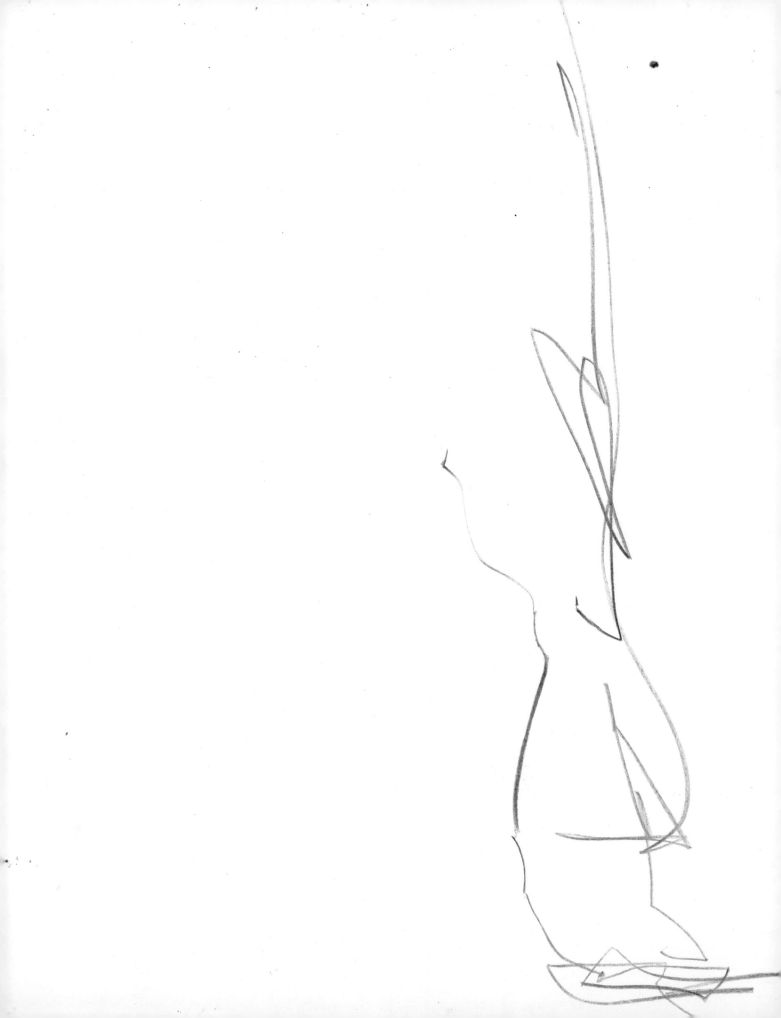